Preface

Isaac Newton, in full Sir Isaac Newton, was an English physicist and mathematician who was the culminating figure of the Scientific Revolution of the 17th century. In optics, his discovery of the composition of white light integrated the phenomena of colors into the science of light and laid the foundation for modern physical optics.

In mechanics, his three laws of motion, the basic principles of modern physics, resulted in the formulation of the law of universal gravitation. In mathematics, he was the original discoverer of the infinitesimal calculus.

With the publication of *Philosophiae Naturalis Principia Mathematica* in 1687, Newton lay the groundwork for modern physics.

Isaac Newton revolutionized our understanding of our world. He was a real Renaissance man with accomplishments in several fields, including astronomy, physics, and mathematics.

Newton gave us new theories on gravity, planetary motion, and optics. It also cemented his position as one of the leading minds of his age.

-**Author**

Sir Isaac Newton
[1642 - 1727]

Isaac Newton was born in the manor house of the tiny village of Woolsthorpe, near Grantham in Lincolnshire, on December 25, 1642. Very small and fragile (small enough to put in a quart pot, so the story told by Newton goes), his life hung in the balance for a week after birth. His father, who had died 3 months

Woolsthorpe Manor-House (Sir Isaac Newton's Birthplace)

before Newton was born, was a yeoman farmer who, if not wealthy, had sufficient means and left a sizeable will. When Newton was 3 years old, his mother remarried the rector Barnabas Smith from the next village 2 km away, leaving Newton to be raised by his grandparents-biographers have expended much ink on the effect this must have had on Newton, who was in adult life a very prickly and insecure character. We know little about Newton's pre-teen years, except that he attended day schools in the neighbouring villages of Skillington and Stoke. In August 1653, when Newton was 10, the Reverend Smith died, and Isaac's mother Hannah returned to Woolsthorpe, having borne 3 children by Barnabas Smith.

Hannah Ayscough

At 12, Newton was sent to grammar school in Grantham. Here he received the formal education of the time, which included Latin and Greek, and Biblical studies - at that time, this meant absorbing the canons of the Anglican Protestant faith. He was placed in the lowest class at Grantham, but as time went on, he rose academically to the top of the school. Apart from a playground fight that he won due to sheer spirit began a rise to the top of the school, Newton kept little company with the other boys of the school- he was a solitary boy, a 'sober, silent, thinking lad', and preferred the company of girls. There was an adolescent romance with a Miss Storer, the stepdaughter of the apothecary Mr. Clark with whom Newton lodged when he was at school in Grantham. This was the only recorded romantic attachment of his life. Most of the stories about Newton recorded at this time in Grantham concern 'his strange inventions and extraordinary inclination for mechanical works'. Amongst these were a windmill powered by a treadmill run by a mouse (the mouse stimulated by pulling a string tied to its tail), various working designs and models for kites, dolls' furniture, and a little four-wheeled vehicle which ran by a crank, which he could turn while sitting in it. He also devised a very large number of sundials, which could be found all over Clark's house, along with many drawings by Newton (mostly of people- he learned to be a proficient draftsman).

In late 1659, when he turned 17, Newton's mother called him home to Woolsthorpe and appointed a servant to teach him about running the farm- this was the vocation intended for him. This did not go well. Sent out to look after the sheep, he spent his time building model waterwheels, dams, and sluices, leaving the sheep to run wild; and when sent to market, he would bribe the servant to go in his place while he spent the day reading or designing various devices. This went on for 9 months until both his uncle William Ayscough (his mother's brother) and his former schoolmaster Mr Stokes stepped in and pressured Newton's mother to send him back to school to prepare for the university. Stokes even agreed to drop the fee for school attendance and to lodge Newton at his own home. Hannah Newton eventually conceded, and he returned to Grantham. Finally, in June 1661, Newton set out for Cambridge- by all accounts, both the servants at Woolsthorpe and the boys at Grantham were glad to see the back of him.

On arrival in Cambridge, Newton entered Trinity College. Then as now, Trinity was the most famous of the Cambridge colleges; and then, as now, life at Trinity reflected rather clearly the mores and class structure of the upper end of English society (by the end of the 20th century, most Oxford and Cambridge colleges were admitting women but in 2004 the

Trinity College, Cambridge

students are still overwhelmingly from the higher strata of British society- over 50% of students from the top 7% of income earners). In Newton's day, Cambridge was almost entirely reserved for the sons of the aristocracy and landed gentry. Newton himself entered Trinity as a subsizar, i.e., a pauper student who earned his keep by performing menial tasks for the fellows, fellow commoners (very rich students), and pensioners (the merely affluent). His mother was not prepared to pay for any more of his education (although she did not lack the means to do so). In those days the syllabus reflected 4 centuries of Aristotelianism, and Cambridge University was not an intellectual centre- it seems that the best one says is that it allowed Newton the time and opportunity to start reading and thinking about a wide variety of subjects. Our best record of these is provided by a diary or notebook he kept, in which his reading was recorded and his thoughts on it. Part of this notebook was entitled "Quaestiones quaedam Philosophical", and we can follow his reading of parts of Galileo, Thomas Hobbes, Henry More, Robert Boyle, and many others, including Plato and Aristotle. He studied Descartes, who was naturally not on any syllabus but whose ideas had already created considerable interest. Newton organised his notes into 45 categories, ranging over questions about the matter, time and place, colours and other sensory qualities, and even occult qualities. Interestingly, his philosophical interests had quickly gravitated towards questions of physics (a subject yet to be clearly defined) and he very quickly found almost any previous philosophy lacking. This is most clear in his extensive notes on Descartes- particularly on Descartes's theory of light and how it accorded with his vortex theory of matter and dynamics in the universe. Newton was fascinated by light and vision at this time, subjecting himself to experiments that could have cost him his sight (these included staring at the sun as long as possible and inserting objects behind his eye as far as he could- in both cases to see the effect on his vision). It seems that sometime in late 1663 Newton also discovered mathematics- a subject not taught at school and barely at university.

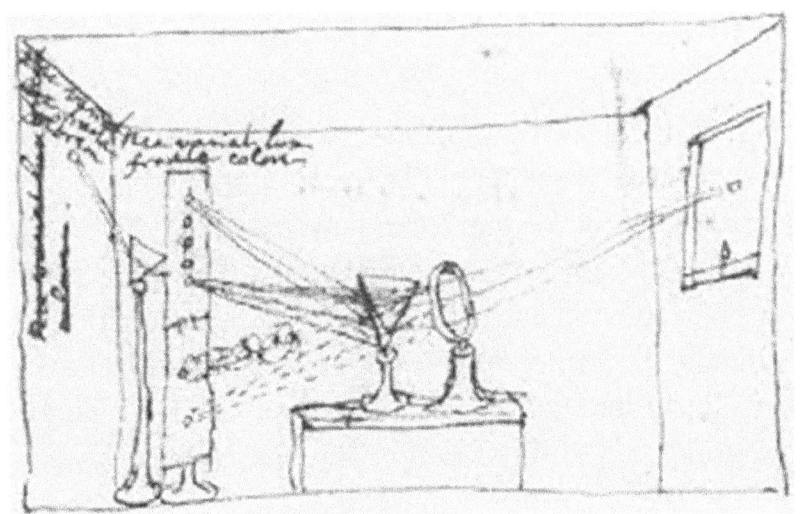

Sketch made by Newton

By 1664 he was buying various advanced books, which by Christmas 1664 included the works of Franz van Schootens, Descartes, and Wallis, on geometry, algebra, and infinite series. During this period, Newton seems to have absorbed much of the mathematics of his day purely by solitary study and become extremely interested in both pure mathematics and how it might be applied to the world. However, a rather important problem had to be resolved at this point. If Newton wished to continue his studies further, he needed to secure a position at Cambridge for a longer time- he had not distinguished himself in his first 3 years of conventional studies. In practice, this meant obtaining a college scholarship, which would give him 4 years more time- but these were fairly competitive (and worse still, more than half of them went to students from the exclusive Westminster school- a concession towards the upper echelons of society which still continues today in some Oxbridge colleges).

Luckily for Newton, he did get the scholarship in April 1664- apparently, either his patron Humphrey Babington helped here, or perhaps the newly arrived Lucasian Professor of Mathematics, Isaac Barrow. The scholarship gave him some financial independence, and he settled in to indulge in further pursuit of his investigations. These were fairly intense since he often went nights without sleep and days without eating. However, within a year, he was forced to quit Cambridge- the Plague arrived in England in 1665, and it was extremely dangerous to stay in cities. Newton left in the early summer, and for 8 months, the university was almost deserted. He returned in March 1666 but left again in June- the Plague had returned. It was not until April 1667 that he was able to return definitively.

During these two years of university closure, Newton returned to Woolsthorpe, to his mother's house. 50 years later, Newton recalled these days- after a description of what he had worked on, he added by way of explanation:

"All of this was in the two plague years of 1665-66. In those days, I was in the prime of my age for invention and minded Mathematicks and Philosophy more than ever."

From these remarks, and similar ones made during the dispute over priority in the invention of calculus, came the legend of Newton's annuls mirabilis. It is probably better seen as a natural result of his current endeavours, which he could pursue more easily because of the leisure afforded by Woolsthorpe. In any case, it is clear that during this time, Newton laid many of the foundations for his later work and, in some cases, came to conclusions that would not be published until 30 years later.

Especially in the earlier part of his life, Newton was a deeply introverted character and fiercely protective of his privacy. Even in his maturity, having become rich, famous, laden with honours and internationally acclaimed as one of the world's foremost thinkers, he remained deeply insecure, given to fits of depression and outbursts of violent temper, and implacable in pursuit of anyone by whom he felt threatened. The most famous example of this is his carefully-orchestrated

Gottfried von Leibniz

campaign to destroy the reputation of Gottfried Leibniz, who he believed (quite unfairly) had stolen the discovery of calculus from him. Yet he was also capable of great generosity and kindness, and there is no lack of tributes to his affability and hospitality, at least in his later years.

His psychological problems culminated in what would now be called a nervous breakdown in mid-1693, when, after five nights of sleeping 'not a wink', he temporarily lost all grip on reality and became convinced that his friends Locke and Pepys were conspiring against him. He later confessed to Locke that during this crisis, 'when one told me you were sickly ... I answered it was better if you were dead' (it is not clear whether Newton really did tell anyone this or merely imagined that he had). He seems, however, to have made a full recovery by the end of the year.

It should be said that such an arrangement was not particularly unusual in the mid-seventeenth century, but that does not in itself rule out the possibility - if not the likelihood - that this early experience of loss and betrayal permanently damaged Newton's capacity for trust and close friendship. It has also been suggested - though this is purely conjectural and much disputed - that he was a repressed homosexual, which, if true, would undoubtedly have placed a man of his background and upbringing under extreme mental strain.

Whatever the reasons, the fact remains that Newton's defensive secretiveness makes it extremely difficult to form a full and balanced assessment of his character. There are no private diaries, and hardly any of his correspondence touches on the details of his private life or state of mind. Though we are lucky to have a substantial collection of second-and third-hand accounts of Newton's early years (see the documents in **Newton as Seen by Others**), only a very few manuscripts in his own hand, dating from his boyhood and undergraduate years, give a more direct insight into his personal world.

By far the most important of these is the list Newton wrote out in 1662 of all the sins he could remember having committed, which he kept up-to-date for an uncertain but fairly short period thereafter (in the **Fitzwilliam Notebook**). Addressed directly to God, this gives a fascinating glimpse into Newton's conscience. Perhaps the most striking feature of the list is how short it is and how innocuous most of the 'sins' now seem. The misdemeanours Newton confessed are far less racy than those recorded in Samuel Pepys's much more famous and substantial diary, but they obviously weighed heavily on him, and he adopted the same strategy as Pepys of writing in shorthand as a sort of code (though in both cases it is a relatively simple code to crack).

It says much about the sternly puritanical cast of Newton's upbringing that many years after the event, he still felt guilty about several minor instances of Sabbath-breaking, including 'Squirting water on Thy day' and 'Making pies on Sunday night'. Other misdeeds seem, to modern secular ears, even more innocuous: 'Idle discourse on Thy day and at other times'; 'Peevishness at Master Clarks for a piece of bread and butter'. Yet there are also hints of the rages and dark depressions that would continue to blight his adult life: 'Striking many'; 'Punching my sister'; 'Wishing death and hoping it to some'.

Nothing else quite so revealingly personal as this survives, but much can be read between the lines of the other private notebooks Newton kept as a schoolboy and undergraduate.

In the Pierpont Morgan Notebook, begun probably in 1659 (two years before Newton went to Cambridge), there are numerous series of words arranged, under a number of subject headings, in quasi-alphabetical order. This was done, presumably, as a handwriting and/or vocabulary-building exercise, and for the most part the lists are copied verbatim from a popular text-book of the day, Francis Gregory's *Nomenclatura brevis anglo-Latino*, but Newton makes some surprising and surely revealing additions of his own. The word 'Father', copied from Gregory, is followed by Newton's own supplement 'Fornicator, Flatterer', while 'Brother', though it is indeed followed by 'Bastard' in Gregory's list, sparked a whole volley of further abusive terms in Newton's mind, including 'Blasphemer', 'Brawler', 'Babler', 'Babylonian', 'Bishop' and ending with 'Benjamite'. A 'Benjamite' was an over-indulged youngest son (about Genesis 42, in which Jacob shows his youngest son Benjamin preferential treatment over his brothers). It is surely significant that Newton's younger half-brother was also called Benjamin.

The other most crucial evidence for an understanding of Newton's development in adolescence and adulthood is supplied by the lists of expenses he kept from 1659-69 in the **Fitzwilliam Notebook** and another one now known as the **Trinity Notebook**. These soften the image of an unsmiling, self-absorbed Puritan Newton by revealing that as an undergraduate, he did get out once in a while to the tavern and the bowling green and even occasionally played cards (and lost). More surprisingly, he appears to have run an informal money-lending operation for fellow students at Cambridge, though whether he charged interest on his loans is unclear.

These notebooks also chart the development of Newton's intellectual interests. His practical bent, which later enabled him to devise and conduct experiments unassisted and to build most of his scientific apparatus himself, is already evident in the **Pierpont Morgan notebook**, the early part of which is crammed with recipes for making paints and medicines and instructions for performing conjuring tricks. In 1669, the expense lists began to fill up with purchases of (al)chemical materials, books and equipment to stock the private laboratory he set up on the grounds of Trinity College. His disillusion with the very conservative curriculum on offer at Cambridge is evidenced by another notebook **(Add. Ms. 3996** in Cambridge University Library), which begins with a series of notes on Aristotle and other orthodox academic sources but then abruptly changes tack and engages actively with the latest theories in science and mathematics, particularly those of Descartes.

Newton's intellectual activities as an undergraduate were almost entirely extra-curricular. His near-total disregard for the subjects he was ostensibly supposed to be studying - primarily the ethics and natural philosophy of Aristotle - actually led to his being regarded as a decidedly poor scholar until his genius was recognised by the mathematics professor Isaac Barrow. But as this notebook proves, he was, in fact, far more in touch with current developments in international scholarship than most of his tutors and professors.

Unfortunately, no such personal material survives - if it ever existed - from the later, more public phase of Newton's career. But the insights these documents offer into his formative years, adolescence and early adulthood make them indispensable to any attempt to form a rounded picture of Newton, the man.

Working on mathematics, Newton began by listing a set of 'problems' which he wanted to investigate- he ended up with 22 of these, grouped into 5 categories. He began by investigating tangents to curves (differentiation) and the 'quadratures' of curves (i.e., the areas under them- now known as 'integration'). With these 'new analyses', he calculated the area under a hyperbola and eventually devised methods to find the area under almost all algebraic curves then known. In the autumn of 1665, he extended these ideas to treat the areas swept out by curves kinetically as areas swept out by a moving point. He used the term 'fluxional' to describe increments of the area in this method- this marks the beginning of the modern version of calculus, and in it, he already saw 'velocity' as a fluxional, defined concerning infinitesimal time intervals- with time defined as an absolute quantity. He then found the relation between integration and differentiation and, in the course of summing various series expansions, found the 'binomial theorem'. In 1666 he returned on 2 occasions to these mathematical questions, and summarised his results in 3 papers- one written on 13 November 1665, entitled "to find ye velocities of bodies by ye lines they describe"; and two more written in 1666, entitled "To resolve problems by motion these following propositions are sufficient". The last of these was written in October 1666 and contained a full description of his theory of calculus.

Newton's mathematical thinking includes the study of Infinite series, Binomial theorem and the evolution of the Differential calculus

His theory of calculus was built on earlier work by his fellow Englishmen John Wallis and Isaac Barrow, as well as on the work of such Continental mathematicians as René Descartes, Pierre de Fermat, Bonaventura Cavalieri, Johann van Waveren Hudde and Gilles

Personne de Roberval. Unlike the static geometry of the Greeks, calculus allowed mathematicians and engineers to make sense of the motion and dynamic change in the changing world around us, such as the orbits of planets, the motion of fluids, etc.

The initial problem Newton was confronting was that, although it was easy enough to represent and calculate the average slope of a curve (for example, the increasing speed of an object on a time-distance graph), the slope of a curve was constantly varying, and there was no method to give the exact slope at any one individual point on the curve i.e. effectively the slope of a tangent line to the curve at that point.

Intuitively, the slope at a particular point can be approximated by taking the average slope ("rise over run") of ever smaller segments of the curve. As the segment of the curve being considered approaches zero in size (i.e. an infinitesimal change in x), then the slope calculation approaches closer and closer to the same slope at a point.

Without going into too much-complicated detail, Newton (and his contemporary Gottfried Leibniz independently) calculated a derivative function $f'(x)$ which gives the slope at any point of a function $f(x)$. This process of calculating the slope or derivative of a curve or function is called differential calculus or differentiation (or, in Newton's terminology, the "method of fluxions" – he called the instantaneous rate of change at a particular point on a curve the "fluxion", and the changing values of x and y the "fluents"). For instance, the derivative of a straight line of the type $f(x) = 4x$ is just 4; the derivative of a squared function $f(x) = x^2$ is $2x$; the derivative of cubic function $f(x) = x^3$ is $3x^2$, etc. Generalizing, the derivative of any power function $f(x) = x^r$ is rx^{r-1}. Other derivative functions can be stated, according to certain rules, for exponential and logarithmic functions, trigonometric functions such as $\sin(x)$, $\cos(x)$, etc., so that a derivative function can be stated for any curve without discontinuities. For example, the derivative of the curve $f(x) = x^4 - 5x^3 + \sin(x^2)$ would be $f'(x) = 4x^3 - 15x^2 + 2x\cos(x^2)$.

Having established the derivative function for a particular curve, it is then an easy matter to calculate the slope at any particular point on that curve, just by inserting a value for x. In the case of a time-distance graph, for example, this slope represents the speed of the object at a particular point.

The "opposite" of differentiation is integration or integral calculus (or, in Newton's terminology, the **"method of fluents"**), and together differentiation and integration are the two main operations of calculus. Newton's Fundamental Theorem of Calculus states that differentiation and integration are inverse operations, so that, if a function is first integrated and then differentiated (or vice versa), the original function is retrieved.

The integral of a curve can be thought of as the formula for calculating the area bounded by the curve and the x axis between two defined boundaries. For example, on a graph of velocity against time, the area "**under the curve**" would represent the distance travelled. Essentially, integration is based on a limiting procedure which approximates the area of a curvilinear region by breaking it into infinitesimally thin vertical slabs or columns. In the same way as for differentiation, an integral function can be stated in general terms: the integral of any power $f(x) = x^r$ is $x^{r+1}/_{r+1}$, and there are other integral functions for exponential and logarithmic functions, trigonometric functions, etc, so that the area under any continuous curve can be obtained between any two limits.

Newton chose not to publish his revolutionary mathematics straight away, worried about being ridiculed for his unconventional ideas, and contented himself with circulating his thoughts among friends. After all, he had many other interests, such as philosophy, alchemy, and his work at the Royal Mint. However, in 1684, the German Leibniz published his independent version of the theory, whereas Newton published nothing on the subject until 1693. Although the Royal Society, after due deliberation, gave credit for the first discovery to Newton (and credit for the first publication to Leibniz), something of a scandal arose when it was made public that the Royal Society's subsequent accusation of plagiarism against Leibniz was authored by none other Newton himself, causing an ongoing controversy which marred the careers of both men.

Sir Isaac Newton

Despite being his best-known contribution to mathematics, calculus was by no means Newton's only contribution. He is credited with the generalized binomial theorem, which describes the algebraic expansion of powers of a binomial (an algebraic expression with two terms, such as $a^2 - b^2$); he made substantial contributions to the theory of finite differences (mathematical expressions of the form $f(x + b) - f(x + a)$); he was one of the first to use fractional exponents and coordinate geometry to derive solutions to Diophantine equations (algebraic equations with integer- only variables); he developed the so-called "Newton's method" for finding successively better approximations to the zeroes or roots of a function; he was the first to use infinite power series with any confidence; etc.

In 1687, Newton published his *"Principia"* or *"The Mathematical Principles of Natural Philosophy"*, generally recognized as the greatest scientific book ever written. In it, he presented his theories of motion, gravity, and mechanics, explained the eccentric orbits of comets, the tides and their variations, the precession of the Earth's axis, and the motion of the Moon.

Mathematics was not the only subject occupying him at that time- in fact, much of his time was spent looking at the problem in mechanics and optics. In the science of mechanics, Descartes had analysed impact in terms of an internal force possessed by a moving body, which he called the 'force of a body's motion'.

Newton instead argues for a cause and effect relation between external forces acting upon a body and changes in its motion. At the same time, he realized that the momentum of two bodies, isolated from each other, would remain constant; even after collisions between them, this would later become the principle of momentum conservation. It might seem from this that Newton had already found his 2nd law of motion. However, at this point, he was confused by the more complex problem of the mechanics of circular motion, and Newton ended up agreeing with Descartes that a body in circular motion strives to constantly recede from the center- which apparently conformed with the Cartesian idea that bodies in motion had their own innate 'centrifugal' force (a name due to Huyghens). Newton calculated the centrifugal force for a circular motion of velocity v at radius r as $F = mv2/r$, and then, recalling his studies of Galileo's "Dialogue Concerning the Two Chief World Systems" he used his result to show that the earth's rotation does not fling bodies into the air because the force of gravity, measured by the rate of fall of falling bodies, is greater than the centrifugal force arising from the earth's rotation. He then went on to show that if he supposed Kepler's 3rd law to be true (that the mean radii R of a planet's orbit is related to its orbital period T by $R \propto T 2/3$), then this implied that the centrifugal force (and hence the force of gravity) must vary like $F \propto 1/R2$. Again, this seems as if he had was very close to finding the universal law of gravitation- but this is to underestimate the leap

Sir Isaac Newton

Isaac Newton experiment with light

required to go from a single result to a total system of dynamics, which would not come until 30 years later. As we shall see below, Newton had to make several huge steps in the intervening period before he would be able to formulate his universal principles of mechanics. During the same enforced stay at Woolsthorpe, Newton continued experimenting with what he called the 'celebrated phenomena of colors' stimulated partly by ideas appearing in the 'Micrographia' published in 1665 by Robert Hooke. Hooke advocated a theory in which colors were a mixture of light and darkness, as well as the idea that light came in 'pulses'; he argued for a scale ranging from brilliant red, which was held to be pure white light, with the least amount of darkness added, to dull blue, the last step before black, which was seen as the complete extinction of light by darkness. Newton realized that this could not be the case - a white page with black writing did not appear colored when viewed from a distance, and the black and white blended- it appeared grey.

At that time, several investigators were using prisms to experiment with color, and the main view was that somehow the prism colored white light from, e.g., the sun. In their experiments, Descartes, Hooke, and Boyle had put a screen close to the prism and saw that a light ray passing through the prism came out as a mixture of colors. In the study upstairs at Woolsthorpe, Newton set up an experiment in which the light beam travelled 22 feet from the window through his prism to project a spectrum on the far wall. The white light split into different colors and each color had been bent a different amount by the prism. He then carried out many experiments on this system. The most crucial of these- what he called his 'Experimentum Crucis'- consisted in putting a screen with a small slit in the way of his spectrum so that only light of one color, eg., blue, passed through to the wall. He then placed a second prism in the path of this blue light. The pure blue light remained unchanged, proving that the prism did not change the colors, thereby making the crucial discovery that white light was simply made from colors mixed together, which the prism could separate. He confirmed this by recombining different colors from 3 different prisms to get white light again.

None of this was able to explain the colors of solid bodies. Newton's efforts in this direction were less successful because he incorrectly believed that these colors were all produced by reflection- that if a body appeared blue, it was because it preferentially reflected blue light. He also investigated a peculiar phenomenon found by Hooke, which was that if a piece of curved glass were put into contact with a flat piece, then one could see very fine rings around the point of contact. this was one of the reasons that Hooke had advocated pulses. Newton was able to give a quantitative treatment of the size of these rings (now known as 'Newton's rings'), knowing the curvature of the curved glass, thereby extracting the length of the pulses. However, he regarded these 'pulses' as being some kind of vibrational disturbance in the medium of corpuscles which made up the light- rather than supposing that the pulse really was light, as Hooke did. From this time on, we see Newton's undeviating belief that light was made from particles.

From 1666 to 1689, Newton was at Cambridge almost continuously. The first problem he faced was the election for a fellowship, which if successful, would give him a permanent place in the college, and the freedom to continue his work. On 2nd October 1667, Newton was elected a fellow of the College of the 'Holy and Undivided Trinity', swearing to 'embrace the true religion of Christ with all my soul' and to 'take holy orders when the time prescribed by these statutes arrives, or resign from the college.' Apart from this, a fellow in those days had little duties- the main thing was to avoid 'the 3 sins of crime, heresy, and marriage'. It seems that Newton continued to use the time- continuing his work on optics and now also turning his attention to alchemy, which would remain an interest of his for at least 30 years. He also withdrew even further into his solitary life. However, during this time, he was drawn into one significant interaction with the outside world. The first Lucasian professor of mathematics at Cambridge, Isaac Barrow, passed on to Newton in early 1669 a new book by Nicholas Mercator, which he had been sent by the mathematician Collins; in this book, Mercator had succeeded in summing a series for the expression $\log(1+x)$. Newton immediately recognized that although other mathematicians had not yet uncovered the very general results for series that he had derived in Woolsthorpe, they soon would. He then sent back, via Barrow, a manuscript entitled "De analysi per aequationes numero infinitorum infinitas" ('On the analysis of infinite series'), detailing his general results. In fact, Barrow had had to put considerable pressure on

Sir Isaac Newton

Newton to send this- Newton's reticence and neurotic desire to avoid public exposure were by this time highly developed. In spite of a request to keep the manuscript private, Collins actually distributed copies of it, and for the first time, mathematicians outside Cambridge began to hear of the young Newton.

Shortly thereafter, in October 1669, Newton became the second-ever Lucasian professor of mathematics. This rather astonishing elevation of Newton to one of only eight such endowed professorships in the university was engineered by Barrow- who stood down from the position in order to move on to a position as chaplain to the king. After this, it was hard for Newton to avoid more contact with the outside world. Collins persisted in asking Newton for contributions and even at one time had in his hands an early draft of the theory of fluxions- but Newton asked for it back and Collins never saw it again.

Newton was greatly influenced by the Hermetic tradition with which he had been familiar since his undergraduate days. Newton, always somewhat interested in alchemy, now immersed himself in it, copying by hand treatise after treatise collating them to interpret their arcane imagery. Under the influence of the Hermetic tradition, his conception of nature underwent a decisive change.

Until that time, Newton had been a mechanical philosopher in the standard 17th- century style, explaining natural phenomena by the motions of particles of matter. Thus, he held that the physical reality of light is a stream of tiny corpuscles diverted from its course by the presence of denser or rarer media. He felt that the apparent attraction of tiny bits of paper to a piece of glass that has been rubbed with cloth results from an ethereal effluvium that streams out of the glass and carries the bits of paperback with it. This mechanical philosophy denied the possibility of action at a distance; as with static electricity, it explained apparent attractions away through invisible ethereal mechanisms. Newton's "Hypothesis of Light" of 1675, with its universal ether, was a standard mechanical system of nature. Some phenomena, such as the capacity of chemicals to react only with certain others, puzzled him, however, and he spoke of a "secret principle" by which substances are "sociable" or "unsociable" with others. About 1679, Newton abandoned the ether and its invisible mechanisms and began to ascribe the puzzling phenomena – chemical affinities, the generation of heat in chemical reactions, surface tension in fluids, capillary action, the cohesion of bodies, and the like – to attractions and repulsions between particles of matter.

More than 35 years later, in the second English edition of Opticks, Newton accepted an ether again, although it was an ether that embodied the concept of action at a distance by posting a repulsion between its particles. The attractions and repulsions of Newton's speculations were direct transpositions of Hermetic philosophy's occult sympathies and antipathies; mechanical philosophers never ceased to protest. Newton, however, regarded them as a modification of the mechanical philosophy that rendered its subject to exact mathematical treatment. As he conceived of them, attractions were quantitatively defined, and they offered a bridge to unite the two basic themes of 17th-century science, the mechanical tradition, which had dealt primarily with verbal mechanical imagery, and the Pythagorean tradition, which insisted on the mathematical nature of reality. Newton's reconciliation through the concept of force was his ultimate contribution to science.

It was Newton's reflecting telescope, the first example of which he had made in 1668, that finally attracted the full attention of the scientific community. He made this first telescope entirely on his own, including the casting of the mirror and with tools that he had devised specifically for the purpose. The first reflecting telescope was only six inches long and one inch in diameter, yet it magnified 40 times. He then made a second more powerful one that could magnify up to 150 times. Newton was sufficiently proud of his telescope that he couldn't resist showing it to others, and eventually, the Royal Society heard of it and asked to see it. When finally Barrow brought it at the end of 1671, it caused a sensation. Within a month, Henry Oldenberg, the secretary of the Royal Society, had communicated the news to Huyghens in Leiden (who was enormously impressed with 'the marvelous telescope of Mr. Newton'), and the Society had elected Newton as a member. Newton was flattered, despite his pretense of indifference, and in return, he communicated details of the operation and construction to Huyghens in several letters- and then finally, after hesitation, sent to the Royal Society his 'Endeavour to testify my gratitude by communicating what my poor and solitary endeavors can effect towards ye promoting your Philosophical designs'. This was his theory of colors, finally sent on 6th February 1672, and which *Oldenberg* then published in 19 February 1672 in the *Philosophical Transactions of the Royal Society*. Newton's description of his telescope appeared in the following issue.

The letter Newton sent contained the results of his investigations and experiments from the Woolsthorpe years, plus an account of how these had helped him design the reflector. It was the first time his work had been made available for open discussion by other scientists. Most initial reactions were very favourable, and queries from the French Jesuit Pardies, professor at the College Louis le Grand (then and now one of the most exclusive prep schools in France), about whether or not the recent discovery by Grimaldi of diffraction should be included in his theory of light, led Newton to articulate his approach to scientific questions in a very interesting passage:

"In answer to this, it is to be observed that the doctrine I explained concerning refraction and colors consists only in certain properties of light, without regarding any hypotheses by which these properties might be explained. The best and safest method of philosophizing seems to be first to inquire diligently into the properties of things, establish those properties by experiment, and then proceed more slowly to hypotheses for the explanation of them. Hypotheses should only be employed in explaining the properties of things but not assumed to determine them unless so far as they may furnish experiments. For if hypotheses can be the test of truth and reality of things, I do not see how certainty can be attained in any science; since numerous hypotheses can be devised, which shall seem to overcome new difficulties. Hence it has been here thought necessary to lay aside all hypotheses, as foreign to this purpose..."

Although Pardies replied that he was satisfied, it is rather hard to believe he could have been reconciled to a methodology so utterly opposed to that of Descartes.

Unfortunately, not all readers did not respond so sympathetically. Robert Hooke, a leading power at the Royal Society, considered optics to be his domain, and in a letter sent only 1 week after Newton's submission, on the 15th Feb 1672, he disdainfully rejected most of Newton's conclusions. The reply from Newton was 4 months in coming- in the interim, he composed a full exposition of his ideas on light, which he then decided not to publish, and contented himself with a vehement attack on Hooke in June. After this, it became more and more difficult to get Newton to respond to letters, although he did for a time respond to letters from Huyghens. At one point, he even threatened to withdraw from the Royal Society- in any case, for some years thereafter, he refused to communicate to anyone directly except for Oldenberg and Collins. This policy he maintained apart from a few departures- most notably to send into the Royal Society in 7th December 1678 2 manuscripts on optics, one entitled "Discourse of Observations", and the other "A hypothesis explaining the properties of light discoursed of in my several papers". The latter was an attempt by Newton, under the stimulus of by then 6 years of letters received from abroad, to give some sort of explanation for the properties of light that he had found. He again expressed his idea that light was a particle, which was guided in its flight by an aether, exerting pressure on the light corpuscles. Homogeneities in the aether explained refraction and reflection, and vibrations in the aether explained the phenomena of 'Newton's rings. He went further, collisions and surface tension were explained by aethereal pressure, and the circular motion of planets in their orbits, and gravitational force in general, came from the pressure of a constant stream of aether which poured into massive bodies. We see that in spite of already knowing of the inverse square law of gravitation, Newton was still under the spell of an almost Cartesian idea of the origin of gravity, and also of light, and rather far from his later theory. His reasons for this point of view were not found in his published work but his unpublished alchemical work.

We've all heard the story. A young Isaac Newton is sitting beneath an apple tree contemplating the mysterious universe.

Suddenly – boink! -an apple hits him on the head.

"Aha!" he shouts, or perhaps, "Eureka!" In a flash he understands that the very same force that brought the apple crashing toward the ground also keeps the moon falling toward the Earth and the Earth falling toward the sun: gravity.

Or something like that. The apocryphal is one of the most famous in the history of science and now you can see for yourself what Newton said.

Newton's Rooms at Trinity with apple tree

Squirreled away in the archives of London's Royal Society was a manuscript containing the truth about the apple.

It is the manuscript for what would become a biography of Newton entitled Memoirs of Sir Isaac Newton's life, written by William Stukeley, an archeologist and one of Newton's first biographers, and published in 1752. Newton told the apple story to Stukeley, who relayed it as such:

"After dinner, the weather being warm, we went into the garden, under the shade of some apple trees... he told me he was just in the same situation as when formerly, the notion of gravitation came into his mind. It was occasioned by the fall of an apple as he sat in a contemplative mood. Why should that apple always descend perpendicularly to the ground, thought he to himself...."

So it turns out the apple story is true – for the most part. The apple may not have hit Newton in the head, but I'll still picture it that way. Meanwhile, three and a half centuries and an Albert Einstein later, physicists still don't understand gravity.

After this, Newton took no real interest in either optics or mechanics for a long time. This was despite seeing, in Sept 1677, two communications sent to Oldenberg from the then young Leibniz, describing Leibniz's mathematical research- from which it would have been obvious to Newton that Leibniz already was well on the way to inventing the calculus independently from Newton. The reason for his neglect is simple- his interests had shifted. During the period 1672-1684, most of Newton's time was consecrated to work on what were quite fundamental questions in theology and alchemy.

It is common amongst interpreters of Newton to neglect or even ignore Newton's work in alchemy and theology completely- pretending that it was either an aberration or, at best irrelevant to his most important work. This view (which is particularly common amongst scientists) makes no sense- and even a mild familiarity with Newton's writings shows that his research into both subjects is related in crucial ways to his work in mechanics and optics. Indeed, in his alchemical research, he was partly looking for underlying explanations and principles which might bear on his discoveries in optics and mechanics; and his theological work was part and parcel of his search for general philosophical principles. To believe that the theory of mechanics embodied in the Principia sprung by magic from the bare philosophical ground is analogous to belief in a virgin birth- and neither belief is reliant on historical fact.

Newton's work in chemistry and alchemy (and the line between the 2 was not even defined in those days) began very early- from his notes, it is known that already in 1669, he was deeply interested in the subject, and by 1672 it already occupied most of his time. In 1669 he purchased 2 ovens, glass equipment, and chemicals in order to begin an experimental programme of research that continued almost unbroken (except for the late 1680s) for over 30 years! At the same time, he had already begun to assemble a set of manuscripts and notebooks, which now constitute most of Newton's surviving papers.

The first sign in any of Newton's infrequent published work of this new interest is to be found in his 1678 works on optics. In his "Hypothesis explaining the properties of light" he postulated a universal aether, whose behaviour was governed by a number of principles- these were divided into active principles like a tendency to condense into massive bodies (the mechanism of gravity) or into fermenting or burning objects- or to be 'exhaled' in the formation of vapours (i.e., vapourisation or boiling). The following passage gives a taste of the ideas- this is a discussion of what are now called phase transitions (e.g., gas/liquid transitions):

"For Nature is a perpetual circulatory worker, generating fluids out of solids, and solids out of fluids, fixed things out of volatile, and volatile out of fixed, subtle out of gross, and gross out of subtle. Some things to ascend and make the upper terrestrial juices, rivers, and the atmosphere; and by consequence others to descend for a Requital to the former"

Remember that this quote is taken from a paper published in the transactions of the Royal Society, whose subject was optics. In some ways, it is not much

Sir Isaac Newton

of an advance over Aristotle- it seems ironic that one of the major themes of debate at this time was over the existence or non-existence of 'occult' qualities in the matter, and perhaps the main proponent of the use of mechanical principles to replace occult ideas was none other than Descartes- e.g., in his theories of vortices to explain magnetic forces and gravitation. Newton was wrestling with precisely the same set of questions, and they were as old as the Greeks- whether to explain dynamics by active or innate principles, whether a void existed and was needed to understand motion, what was the fundamental substance or substances and in what way were they manifested in the ever-changing. properties of visible matter. It is crucial to understand that Newton and Descartes were working in an intellectual framework no different from their forbears. For both of them, as for many others, it was then natural to look upon the phenomena of magnetism and gravity as unusually interesting, along with the properties of light- in all 3 cases, one was dealing with invisible influences acting at a distance. The temptation to find something common between these phenomena and look for some hidden substance to explain the transmission of these influences would have been very hard to resist.

In Newton's case, it is quite clear what was going on in his unpublished alchemical work. Having come to what was simply a preliminary and very partial understanding of some mechanical phenomena and some features of light, he was after a deeper and non-mechanical explanation of these properties. Such a search made sense; how could mechanical models explain phenomena like magnetism and gravity, clearly non-mechanical?

It is interesting to contrast the views of both Newton and his contemporary Robert Boyle (sometimes called the father of modern chemistry) with the standard alchemical views of that time. The standard alchemical system treated Nature as a living principle, not as mechanical- this was Aristotelian- with an activating spirit, such that all things were generated by the fusion of 'male and female principles'. In 17th century Europe this was mixed up with Christian philosophical ideas dating back to the 4th century, concerning the Holy Trinity- thus Effararius, the Monk, identified three basic activating principles, which were body, soul, and spirit (with the body being feminine Venus, spirit being masculine Mars, and soul being identified with sun and moon). These activating principles existed in a matter; they were causative agents responsible for change- and there was a widespread belief in one pure or fundamental agent manifested in what was known as the 'philosopher's stone'. Because this agent was capable of causing a change in matter, it was eagerly sought after by alchemists (by some, for the purpose of transmuting base metals into gold). In terms of such ideas, phenomena such as the solubility of some materials in others, or vaporization, were explained

Sir Isaac Newton

by the sympathy or antipathy of some principles for others. Thus the dissolving of a substance in a solvent was explained as the 'sympathy between the substance and its menstrum.

Boyle, on the other hand, sought underlying mechanical explanations for chemical phenomena- in size and shapes of particles and pores. Newton was having none of this- he postulated a secret alchemical principle, the 'sociability' of some materials for others. Thus the insolubility of water in oil (and vice-versa) but its solubility in wine were to be explained. Thus also was gravity to be explained by the sociability of aether for massive bodies. In correspondence with Boyle over several years, Newton discussed these ideas to cover a very broad range of physical phenomena. In a manuscript begun in 1679, he elaborated his ideas in more detail. This work, "De Aere et Aethere", attempted to understand physical phenomena such as capillary action, vapourization, and the expansion of gases, by appealing to the repulsion between most bodies. For Newton, this repulsion was a fundamental part of his system- it came from the existence of a hard nucleus in material bodies, surrounded by a sphere of more tenuous matter, which did not admit other matter. He also attempted to treat 'electric and magnetic effluvia' with these ideas. Newton was both driven and harnessed by his experimental work in all of this theoretical speculation.

This was extraordinarily extensive, but little of it appeared in his published work. Much of it is very hard to read now- in the absence of any understanding of the elements, how atoms form ions and bond in various ways to form molecules, etc., chemical phenomena were analyzed in terms of 'combination of liquors', which were infused with various spirits, which were more or less sociable with others, etc. Often certain compounds or solutions of compounds were identified as being somehow basic or elemental when in fact, they were complex transient forms of what are now known to be the basic elements. All this led to enormous confusion and a proliferation of names and technical terms describing things that either do not exist at all or are, in reality, composites of more basic things. This shows what happens when the basic taxonomy of a subject is flawed.

Nevertheless, some of this work is fascinating. One of these experiments may have played a crucial role in subsequent developments (although the historical record is insufficiently complete to decide). To understand the interaction between aether and matter, Newton set out to measure the resistance that aether caused to the pendulum's motion. The experiment was simple in conception but hard to do accurately. A long (11 ft. long) pendulum was made with a large wooden box as the weight. This box could be filled with extra weights, giving it extra mass and lessening the effect of air resistance on its motion. Newton then used the theoretical result of Galileo, that without interaction with the aether, the period of motion would be unaffected by the extra weight. By measuring heavier

Sir Isaac Newton

and heavier masses, he sought to find the contribution of the aether to the frictional relaxation of the pendulum motion (assuming it would affect heavier masses less). Of course, the difficulty in experimenting was to eliminate all other sources of friction so that only resistance from the aether was left. The interest of this experiment is that he found no discernable contribution from the aether- the decay of the pendulum oscillations was almost independent of the weight of the box, within very small errors. Thus despite his theoretical prejudice, Newton decided there was no measurable interaction between matter and aether. It is not clear how much of a direct role this played in Newton's later thinking, but it certainly must have influenced his later rejection of the aether.

Newton kept his theological ideas very much to himself- much of what we know has only been uncovered in the last 30 years. It seems as though his interest was awakened in the early 1670s, and by 1674, he was very heavily involved. Again, his interest in theological matters was not the aberration of an eccentric but followed naturally from his desire to get to the bottom of things and discover fundamental truths about the world. It is also argued by some historians that his interest in these questions was precipitated by the necessity for a fellow of Trinity College to be ordained into the Anglican Church and to affirm his orthodox religious beliefs- in Newton's case, this had to be done by 1675, or he would lose his livelihood as a fellow of the college.

Whatever the truth may be, well before 1675, Newton had come to conclusions about the church's doctrines that were heterodox in the extreme. His essential conclusion was that in the 4th century battle between the beliefs of Arius (according to whom God was one, and Jesus only a prophet or mediator) and those of Athanasius (who argued for the Holy Trinity of God, Jesus, and the Holy Spirit), the entire Christian doctrine had been corrupted by the victory of Athanasius. For Newton, this was extremely serious- the worship of Jesus as the son of God, or as part of God, was a form of superstitious idolatry, which for him was sinful. It had, in his opinion, opened the way to a host of false saints and martyrs, the concentration of power in a religious hierarchy and the perversion of monasticism. Newton was led by his historical research to the idea that the true religion was that of Noah, before the corruption of Athanasius and the council of Nicaea in 380 AD; that ancient people had all worshipped gods, but that these were basically the same god under different names. Many of his ideas on this were written down in a manuscript entitled "Theologia gentilis origines philosophicae" (the philosophical origins of gentile theology) around 1684.

To a modern reader, much of this may seem to be rather obscure, and it is perhaps hard to understand why Newton was so exercised by such questions. This is merely a measure of how much the world has changed since the 17th century- Newton was living in the wake of a thousand years of dogmatic religion, which had entirely shaped the European society of his day- he could be no more free from the ideology of his day than we are of ours. In Newton's case, his ideas led him to what was a shattering conclusion for someone in his position- not only that the Christian doctrines of his day were corrupt, but that Christianity itself had nothing, in particular, to distinguish it from other religions. It seems from his writings that he became an Arian (i.e., a follower of Arius) but that apart from a few discussions with very close acquaintances (amongst whom the philosopher John Locke occupied an almost unique place) he kept his beliefs utterly secret.

It is easy to imagine Newton, under different circumstances, becoming a religious figure himself, even a prophet of sorts. His sincere attempts to come to terms with religious doctrine were not distinct from his work on 'Natural Philosophy' but merely the inevitable result of a search for philosophical truth, wherever this might lead. In Newton's day, such a search could hardly lead elsewhere but to an inquiry into religious truth. The remarkable thing is that he was able to keep his ideas secret. The moment of truth came when he had to be ordained into the Anglican Church. We have no first-hand documentation of what happened, but it seems that Newton must have spoken with someone (probably Isaac Barrow, by now Master of Trinity college); we have no idea what was said. On

27 April 1675, a Royal dispensation was granted in perpetuity to the Lucasian Professor (not to Newton), allowing exemption from the taking of Holy Orders if so desired by the said Professor. Thus Newton avoided expulsion from the college only a month before the deadline for ordination.

It is possible to imagine Newton's research into theology and alchemy continuing for many years after the time of his most intense interest in these subjects, in the late 1670s and early 1680s. As we have seen, he was animated by a desire in his alchemical work to get find a non-mechanical theory which would explain the known phenomena of mechanics, optics, and chemistry, and his attention was focused on explanations in terms of an aether, having various 'occult' (i.e., 'hidden') properties of a 'pre- mechanical' kind. Since he showed no desire to publish any of this work or even to share it informally, it is unlikely that Newton would have been more than a footnote in history had things continued in this way.

However, fate intervened, and a sequence of events in the years 1680-84 would set him off on an entirely different course. This led him to completely revise his ideas and culminated in a quite extraordinarily intense outburst of creativity, in which he constructed a philosophical and mathematical system of mechanics, devoid of any aether and quite different from his previous ideas. This theory was embodied in the "Philosophiae Naturalis Principia Mathematica" ('The

Mathematical Principles of Natural Philosophy), written during 1686-87. None of this story is simple, and it also involves the intervention of other key personalities at certain stages. However, the final result was quite astounding, and the 'Principia" is rightly argued by many historians to have been one of the most crucial developments in the history of the world.

By the late 1670's Newton had more or less withdrawn from contact with most of the world- his contact with Oldenberg (secretary of the Royal Society) ceased at the latter's death in Sept. 1677, and in spring 1679, his mother died. Apart from occasional correspondence with Boyle, the affairs of Trinity College (by then in serious financial trouble), and dealing with his mother's estate, Newton's time was completely taken up by his private research work.

The road that led to the Principia began with a correspondence initiated by Robert Hooke (secretary of the Royal Society) in late 1679. Hooke asked Newton about his ideas of orbital motion (which he had first sketched in 1674). In this question, Hooke was the first to make the correct assumption that the motion of a body about, say, the earth, would be governed by its initial rotation, plus the influence of a centrally attractive force, varying like $1/r^2$, where r was the distance from the earth's centre. At no point did Hooke assume any outward centrifugal force (the name given by Huyghens), which everyone had supposed up to that time (including Newton, who had always assumed 2 matching inward and outward forces for circular motion). As noted by Newton, the question can be checked experimentally by dropping the ball from a high tower. However, in a mistake that Newton would severely regret, he answered Halley that the motion would be a kind of spiral falling towards the Earth's centre- to which Hooke responded, in a subsequent exchange of letters, that he thought it would, on the contrary, be an ellipse, assuming the $1/r2$ attraction (this is the correct answer).

Newton quickly realised his mistake- and a few months later worked out the correct theory (without sending it to Hooke). At the time, he did not follow this up-but the issues would not go away- shortly thereafter, in Nov 1680, a spectacular comet appeared in the sky, exciting the interest of many, including Newton; and another followed it in 1682 (what Halley later realised had to be periodic- it is now called Halley's comet and returns every 76 years). It appears from Newton's notes and observations of these comets that he slowly came to the realisation that the cometary dynamics could be understood in the same way as planetary motion- this appears to be the first step on the road to the idea of universal gravitation.

In January 1684, an interesting discussion at the Royal Society in London between Edmund Halley, Robert Hooke, and Christopher Wren. The topic was celestial mechanics, and Hooke asserted to the other two that he could demonstrate all celestial dynamics starting

Sir Isaac Newton

from an inverse square attraction- but that he would not yet reveal his proof. Consequently, Halley asked Newton eight months later, on a visit to Cambridge, what would be the motion of an object in such a force field. As Halley recounts, Newton immediately answered that it would be an ellipse- which he knew because he had calculated it. Halley asked for details, which Newton promised he would send. What he sent in November 1684 was an elaboration of his notes from 1680- in a 9-page manuscript, he demonstrated that a $1/r2$ attraction would lead to motion along a conic section (i.e., an ellipse, parabola, or hyperbola), proved Kepler's 2nd and 3rd laws, and treated the motion of a projectile through a resistive medium.

Halley immediately realised that he was dealing with merely a small part of what Newton must know and immediately returned to Cambridge to ask Newton to elaborate on his short manuscript, which Newton had entitled "De motu corporum in gyrum" (On the motion of bodies in orbit). As reported by Halley to the Royal Society on 10 Dec 1684, Newton agreed to do this. It is unlikely that either Halley or Newton realised at that time what this would lead to.

From Aug 1684-spring 1686, Newton almost ceased all communication with the outside world. There were key exchanges with Flamsteed, through which one can measure his progress in the rewriting of our understanding of Nature, and there were repeated discussions and exchanges with Halley, who was determined by any means to get Newton to publish the full extent of his work. The result of Halley's prodding was to push Newton gradually into a deeper and deeper refinement of the results in his original 9-page manuscript. This began with a series of attempts to revise the manuscript, as Newton tried to refine his ideas, make them more rigorous, and, most importantly, give them some philosophical underpinning.

This last philosophical endeavour motivated Newton to find a framework in which all dynamics could be derived- without such a framework, it was clear that physics could be no more than a piecemeal collection of results having no sure foundation. He began with the existence of what he called 'centripetal' forces (in contrast to the centrifugal force discussed by Huyghens) and a preliminary version of what later became the first law. Dissatisfied, he produced a 2nd version in which 5 laws of dynamics appeared, including the relation between applied force and change of motion- what we now call the 2nd law. In a 3rd version, he introduced the idea of absolute space (which is no longer used in physics- more on this below). It was quite clear what the two most difficult steps were for Newton by this time. He had dropped the whole idea of an aether- this was a huge step and forced him inevitably to the idea of forces acting at a distance through the vacuum- there was no other way to explain planetary motion once the aether had been dropped. The assumption of such an idea must have been extraordinarily difficult, and yet he had been driven to it by all his investigations over the previous years. Having made it, he was then faced with another huge problem- how to deal with the idea of 'inherent force', which was viewed as the internal force a body possesses which keeps it moving in the same direction and speed in the absence of an external force. To us, this seems completely misguided- but at the time, Newton was working in a framework, which had begun with Aristotle, in which the dynamical properties of a body were inherent in the body- a framework which, up to this point, Newton had accepted along with everyone else.

Newton's struggles with inherent force can be observed by looking at his various attempts to formulate what eventually became his first law. His first attempt formulates it as follows:

'The inherent, innate, and essential force of a body is the power by which it perseveres in its state of resting or moving uniformly in a right line, and is proportional to the quantity of the body. It is actually exerted proportionally to the change of state, and in so far as it is exerted, it can be called the exerted force of a body...'

and we see the way in which already the connection to the future 2nd law is being made. In a second attempt he wrote:

'a body, by its "vis inertiae" (force of inertia) alone, perseveres in its state of resting or uniform motion' where the force of inertia is just another name for 'inherent force'.

Eventually, in his final formulation of the 1st law of the Principia, all reference to an inertial force would be dropped. However, even in the Principia, Newton could not relinquish the idea that there was something unique about a state of rest, even in the vacuum-the concepts of Absolute space and Absolute Time appear still. Thus 'absolute motion' would be defined concerning Absolute space. Newton was never able to accept what was, in fact, the inevitable consequence of his formulation- that motion was relative, that no frame of reference was preferred, and that the 1st law was merely a special case of the 2nd, in the absence of any external force. Newton was never happy with the idea of forces transmitted through the vacuum, and he regarded the idea that motion was purely relative as being both atheistic and Cartesian!

For Newton, the formulation of the 2nd law was easy- indeed, he had done it already many years before. What was less trivial was to give a proper definition of mass. This he inevitably did in terms of inertia:

'The inherent force of matter' is the power of resisting by which anybody, as much as in it lies, perseveres in its state of resting or moving uniformly in a right line; and it is proportional to its body and does not differ at all from the inactivity of the mass except in our mode of conceiving it. A body exerts this force only in a change of state effected by another force impressed upon it, and its exercise is 'resistance' and 'impetus' which are distinct only about each other.'

Later Newton would attempt to clarify by explaining that the total mass of a body was the volume times the density (which of course merely displaced the problem to one of defining the density). For a more modern understanding of how one should understand 'mass' in the 2nd law, go to the section on Newtonian mechanics. Finally, the initial formulation of the 3rd law was essentially completed in these initial attempts to rewrite his original manuscript for Halley. He formulated it thus:

'As much as any body acts on another so it experiences in reaction...the force of the body exerted to conserve its state is the same as the force impressed on the other body to change its state, and the change of state of the first body is proportional to the first force, and the second body to the second force.'

This concludes the dynamical part of Newton's theory. At the same time, he was coming slowly to the idea of universal gravitation. This seems to have begun both with his knowledge of planetary motions and his understanding of his pendulum experiments- Newton was inevitably led to understand that if masses were attracted to the earth by force proportional to their mass (as demonstrated by the equal period of pendula with different masses, or the equal rate of fall of different masses), then the same could be true of celestial bodies, including not only the planets but their moons. Using the $1/r2$ law, he could then verify that this was the case, provided the 2nd law was assumed-the periods of the planetary orbits could be calculated accurately without knowing their masses. It was then quite inevitable, once the 3rd law was accepted, that if the sun attracted the Earth or Jupiter, they must also attract the sun and affect its motion (although by a very small amount). In this way, the hypothesis of universal gravitation emerged- that all massive bodies exerted a gravitational force proportional to their mass and fell off as the square of the distance away from them. As Newton put it:

'The forces proportional to the quantity of matter arise from the universal nature of matter'

Thus was a new structure for the world slowly born in early 1685- by gradual attempts to free the mind from the constraints of an older structure.

By early summer 1685, Newton was sufficiently happy with his basic formulation that he was ready to work out some of its consequences. This was quite crucial- his formulation of the laws had emerged from his studies of various specific but limited problems such as planetary or pendulum motion, and for his satisfaction, he had to see that it worked for all dynamic systems. All of Newton's previous investigations, over the 20 year period since his work in Woolsthorpe, now came to the fore- we see how essential this gestation period was for the production of the Principia. In the next 6 months, the original revisions for Halley expanded to 2 books, which Newton entitled "De motu corporum" (The motion of Bodies); no longer was he dealing with planetary motion. In these books, he dealt with the following crucial problems (amongst others):

- *The gravitational attraction exerted by a sphere of uniform density:* The essential point was to show that the force towards the centre of the sphere, on any body outside the sphere, would be proportional to 1/r2. More generally one can show this if the density is inhomogeneous, provided it only depends on the distance from the centre of the sphere. In this way Newton could justify all calculations that treated the earth's gravitational force as though it came from the centre- a quite crucial result. He was then later able to look at small deviations from the sphericity of the earth in a result which turned out to be important; he calculated from the measured results for falling bodies that the earth was an oblate spheroid, with an equatorial diameter of roughly 30 km greater than the polar one (see Principia vol III, propositions XIX, XX). The polar flattening is thus very small, only 1 part in 400; the earth's diameter is roughly 12,000 km. For a time afterwards, French astronomers claimed the opposite (an equatorial flattening), but this was eventually understood to be incorrect.

- *The mutually perturbing effects of the planets:* This is caused by the gravitational interactions between the planets during their motion around the sun. Even though these perturbations are small compared to the huge gravitational force of the sun, they are easily seen by watching planetary motions over a long time. This was a very hard problem; eventually, Newton settled for an approximate treatment of the 3-body problem (i.e., the motion of 2 planets around the sun, with interactions between them included) and was able to show how, e.g., Saturn would be alternately slowed and then speeded up as Jupiter caught up with it and passed ahead of it. We now know that an exact treatment of even this problem is impossible- that the 3-body Newtonian system can be chaotic. This understanding only came in the 20th century- before this the problem of the long-time dynamics of planetary orbits, and their stability, was a central problem in astronomy and mathematics.

-   *Stability of orbits:* even though he was not able to deal with the 3-body problem, Newton could show that for the 2-body problem (e.g., the sun and a single planet) there were only two possible laws of gravitational attraction that would lead to elliptic orbits- one being the usual $F \sim 1/r2$ law, in which attraction falls off as the inverse square of distance, and the other being the harmonic attraction, in which attractive force increases in proportion to the distance, i.e., $F \sim r$. He also found that for these laws the orbits were stable, i.e., that the orientation of the ellipses in place, their size, etc., would not change in time.

- *The Tides, and precession:* This is also a very complex problem, which Newton could not solve fully. Interestingly he dealt with tides in terms of a belt of fluid around the earth, which was deformable- and then by making this belt or ring solid, he was able to deal with the precessional motion of the earth (i.e., the slow motion of the orientation of the earth's axis of rotation- which takes 25 years to complete a single cycle). Knowledge of the shape of the earth is of course necessary to determine the precessional motion, and fine oscillatory corrections to it (known as 'nutation'); this is now completely understood using Newtonian dynamics.

- *The moon's orbit:* This is a very complex 3-body problem, since it involves the sun perturbing the motion of the moon in its orbit around the earth. Newton probably spent more time on this than any other problem- and indeed he found a result for the progression of the apsides, caused by the sun, which was half of the correct observed value, and which caused him great frustration (he was never able to resolve this problem). In the centuries that followed more and more sophisticated attacks were made on the orbital and rotational dynamics of the moon, including its tidal interactions with the sun and the earth- we now have a complete understanding of this.

- *Frictional motion through a medium:* Newton concentrated particularly here on the motion of projectiles through air and fluids, and on the damping of pendulum motion by air. By assuming various dependences on velocity for the dissipation of the motion he was able to give an accurate treatment of the decay of pendulum motion and the slowing down of projectiles.

- *Motion of fluids:* Newton began an attack on what became a crucial part of physics- the propagation of disturbances on fluids and elastic media like solids (including air). His treatment dealt with the velocity of waves and their dependence on the fluid density, their direction of propagation, the oscillation of fluid in pipes, and so on. His treatment was correct, and the formulation of the physics of a fluid as a collection of particles was similar to that of Descartes and others. However he was not willing to go as far as Huyghens, and treat light in this manner (this is discussed in the section on Optics).

- *Vortices, and motion in a fluid vortex:* This last problem was a key problem, since Descartes had argued for a theory in which celestial motions are controlled by a medium in which vortices are centred on massive bodies like the sun, and continental physicists like Huyghens followed

Descartes in this. Newton showed first that the vortex motion of a fluid was unstable, and would decay; and then that the motion of an object in a vortex was such that its orbital period T would vary like the square of the distance from the vortex centre (ie., $T \sim r\ 2$), instead of Kepler's result that $T \sim r\ 2/3$ (which latter of course Newton could establish from the $1/r2$ law of gravitation). This was a fatal blow to the Cartesian theory.

By Nov 1685 these 2 books were finished- after revisions and further expansions, they would become the first 2 volumes of the Principia; on 21st April 1686, Halley was able to inform the Royal Society that the manuscripts were nearly ready, and on 19 May 1686, the Society voted to print them. However, at this point, two problems arose. The first arose because the Royal Society was almost bankrupt- and so on 2nd June, they asked Halley to pay for the printing costs. The second arose because Hooke asked that he be properly referenced in work. This caused a huge dispute between Newton and Hooke and almost caused Newton to abandon the 3rd volume, which he had already begun. By a mixture of flattery and persuasive common sense, Halley managed to convince Newton to eventually finish the 3rd volume- however, instead of being the expected interpretation of the work for the less mathematical reader, Newton turned it into a highly technical treatment of lunar dynamics, with a partial treatment of cometary motion- only in the opening passages do we find any relic of the original more philosophical discussion originally envisaged, along with the following admonition:

"It remains that, from the same principles, I now demonstrate the frame of the System of the World. Upon this subject I had, indeed, composed the 3rd book in a popular method, that it might be read by many; but afterward, considering that such as had not sufficiently into the principles could not easily discern the strength of the consequences, nor lay aside the prejudices which for many years they had been accustomed, therefore to prevent the disputes which might be raised on such accounts, I chose to reduce the substance of this book into the form of Propositions (in the mathematical way), which should be read by those only who had first made themselves masters of the principles established in the preceding books..."

Rarely have the feelings of a scientist wishing to avoid the oversimplification or popularisation of his work been expressed more clearly. Newton largely succeeded in his goal- he was interpreted first by other scientists so that when philosophers like Voltaire came to try and understand him, most of the questions of principle had already been debated by people who at least understood what Newton was saying. This prevented the popular reaction that he feared, for many of the ideas in the Principia were strong stuff- universal gravitation and action at a distance through a vacuum in particular excited a violent reaction from the continent and were not fully accepted in France for a century after that.

When one comes to look at the final published version of the Principia there is precious little of what we would now call philosophy. In the preface to the first book, Newton lists 8 definitions. For example-

"Definition I: The quantity of matter is the measure of the same, arising conjointly from its density and its bulk"

"Definition V: A centripetal force is that by which bodies are drawn or impelled, or in any way tend, towards a point as to a centre" and so on.

There is also an introductory Scholium, in which Absolute time and space, and by contrast, relative motion, are discussed, and an introductory section in which he lists his 'Axioms', or laws of motion, along with lengthy explanations. Finally, in Book III, there is a short discussion of rules of reasoning and a Scholium at the very end 12, whose purpose is to extol the virtues of the creator of the wonderful system of the world, which is revealed to us in the dynamics of bodies. But this is all; for the most part, the Principia is what Newton called Philosophy and Mathematics (and what we would now call classical physics).

During the writing and publication of the Principia, great political events began to shape the future of the British Isles. As the reign of Charles II drew to a close, his power over Parliament had increased to the extent that when Charles died in 1685, his avowedly Catholic brother James was able to ascend the throne (despite votes against such a succession by 3 earlier parliaments). By this time, prominent Protestant intellectuals (such as John Locke) and politicians had already begun to take refuge in anticipation of the coming storm. However, James acted too quickly and foolishly, attempting within a year to overturn the 'Test Acts', install Catholics in many high offices, and order the proclamation in all churches of 'liberty of conscience to all dissenters' in 1687, and again in 1688. On May 18, 1688, James ordered the imprisonment of the Archbishop of Canterbury and 6 other bishops for refusing to do this- but they were acquitted by a jury. This set off riots in the streets, with the burning of the Pope in effigy. It also led to the secret invitation by the 'Immortal 7' (Admiral Edward Russell, the Bishop of London, and 5 peers), extended to Prince William III of Orange, Captain-General of the United Dutch republic, to come to England to preserve the country against the Papist forces. This move seems bizarre, but William was married to Mary, James's first daughter by his 1st marriage; and William was also a grandson of Charles I, executed in 1649.

The birth of a son to James II on June 10, 1688, precipitated the subsequent events. On November 1, 1688, William ordered a Dutch armada to sea. This suicidal mission succeeded- extraordinarily, with no bloodshed. William, aided by fog, succeeded in landing in Exeter- and in the ensuing weeks, many of the English forces, and much of the British Navy, went over to William's side. James, not a courageous man, finally fled to France- and William arrived just before Christmas in London to take over the throne- this was the 'Glorious Revolution'. Thereby began a long-lived alliance of the Netherlands and England against France (which manifested itself in the following years in the 'War of the Spanish Succession', in which the 'Grand Alliance' of England, Austria, the Netherlands, and most German states ranged itself against Louis XIV). The ensuing changes in the British Isles were fundamental. Refugees such as Locke returned from refuge in the Netherlands (Locke in 1689 on the same ship that carried Queen Mary), and from this time on, strife shifted irreversibly to the European continent- to continue on and off until the present day. In 1707 England and Scotland united in the 'Act of Union', and the Parliamentary government has prevailed, without civil war, since that time. This allowed the UK to turn its attention to developing what became the 'British Empire'; and it left scientists and other intellectuals free to pursue their research, largely free from religious interference.

Newton himself lived for another 41 years after finishing the Principia and had an interesting career, which involved him quite prominently in public life, most notably as Master of the Royal Mint. In the 6 years after Principia, he was involved in fairly strenuous intellectual work, but most of this consisted in putting into a coherent form work in alchemy, optics, and mathematics which he had previously done. At the same time, he emerged from his shell and began to cultivate relationships with various people, including John Locke and Christiaan Huyghens (who visited him several times in London). In 1693-4, he suffered a nervous breakdown, the details of which are still not completely known or understood. After this, his creative new work ceased, although he later published quite a lot of older work (including finally, in 1704, the results of his research in optics, much of which had been done 30 years before). The work on optics, published as "Opticks", was written in English rather than Latin, and in a way which made it much more accessible. As a result it became very well-known, and many in the London intelligentsia were led to try and repeat some of the more amusing experiments recounted in it. A detailed description of Newton's optical work, along with that of Huyghens, is given in another section (on opticks).

Newton made the discoveries and waited for people to discover it. The writings of Sir Isaac Newton were a remarkable note to let the world appraise his theories and discoveries. Amongst them few are as follows…

- ➤ The Principia in 1687
- ➤ Opticks in 1704
- ➤ Observations upon the prophecies of Daniel, and the Apocalypse of St. John in 1733
- ➤ The Chronology of Ancient Kingdoms Amended in 1728

- The preliminary manuscripts for Isaac Newton's 1687 Principia, in 1684-1685
- Method of Fluxions in 1736
- An Historical Account of Two Notable Corruptions of Scripture in 1754
- Arithmetica Universalis in 1707
- De mundi systemate 1687
- De motu corporum in gyrum
- Newton's Philosophy of Nature Selections from his Writings
- Principia: "The Mathematical Principles of Natural Philosophy
- Principia, Vol. II: The System of the World
- The Laws of Gravitation
- Newton's System of the World
- New theory about light and colors
- New theory about light and colors
- Notes on the Jewish Temple
- The Mathematical Papers of Isaac Newton: Volume 8
- Isaac Newton: Eighteenth Century Perspectives
- Four Letters from Sir Isaac Newton to Doctor Bentley: Containing Some Arguments in Proof of a Deity

  and many more…

Let's have a look at some of the most famous quotes by Sir Isaac Newton which are not only inspirational and motivating but also prophetic in nature.

○ *If I have seen further it is by standing on the shoulders of Giants.*

○ *I can calculate the motion of heavenly bodies but not the madness of people.*

○ *Men build too many walls and not enough bridges.*

○ *Tact is the knack of making a point without making an enemy.*

○ *What we know is a drop, what we don't know is an ocean.*

○ *Nature is pleased with simplicity. And nature is no dummy*

○ *Gravity explains the motions of the planets, but it cannot explain who sets the planets in motion.*

○ *Truth is ever to be found in the simplicity, and not in the multiplicity and confusion of things.*

○ *And to every action there is always an equal and opposite or contrary, reaction.*

○ *This most beautiful system of the sun, planets and comets, could only proceed from the counsel and dominion of an intelligent and powerful Being.*

Isaac Newton English School 1715

○ *A man may imagine things that are false, but he can only understand things that are true.*

○ *No great discovery was ever made without a bold guess.*

○ *What goes up must come down.*

- *He who thinks half-heartedly will not believe in God; but he who really thinks has to believe in God.*

- *If I have ever made any valuable discoveries, it has been due more to patient attention, than to any other talent.*

- *To myself I am only a child playing on the beach, while vast oceans of truth lie undiscovered before me.*

- *Yet one thing secures us what ever betide, the scriptures assures us that the Lord will provide.*

- *To explain all nature is too difficult a task for any one man or even for any one age*

- *Gravity explains the motions of the planets, but it cannot explain who set the planets in motion.*

- *If I have done great things it's because I was standing in the closet of smart men taking notes and then publishing their ideas as my own.*

- *It is much better to do a little with certainty & leave the rest for others that come after than to explain all things by conjecture without making sure of any thing.*

- *This most elegant system of the sun, planets, and comets could not have arisen without the design and dominion of an intelligent and powerful being.*

Sir Isaac Newton

In 1696 he left Cambridge for London to take up a bureaucratic position, apparently with no regrets-Cambridge had done no more than provide him with a hiding place and the leisure to work uninterrupted but little intellectual stimulus. In 1703 he was elected President of the Royal Society, and in 1705 he was knighted by Queen Anne. Until his death in 1727, Newton was lionized both by society and the international scientific community, even despite the various disputes he got himself into (particularly with Leibniz over the invention of the calculus) and his often dictatorial character. At his death, he was buried in a state funeral in Westminster Abbey- a rare honour for a mere scientist! It was this recognition, according to the author of perhaps the most important contribution made by a single person to the history of human thought, that so impressed the young Voltaire during his 3-year visit to England and Voltaire later became one of Newton's champions for the Enlightenment, fighting against the 'Establishment' of churchmen and 'philosophes', in 18th century France.

In London, Newton assumed the role of patriarch of English science. In 1703 he was elected President of the Royal Society. Four years earlier, the French Académie des Sciences (Academy of Sciences) had named him one of eight foreign associates. In 1705 Queen Anne knighted him, the first occasion a scientist was so honoured. Newton ruled the Royal Society magisterially. John Flamsteed, the Astronomer Royal, had to feel that he ruled it tyrannically. In his years at the Royal Observatory at Greenwich, Flamsteed, a difficult man in his own right, had collected an unrivalled body of data. Newton had received needed information from him for the Principia, and in the 1690s, as he worked on the lunar theory, he again required Flamsteed's data. Annoyed when he could not get all the information he wanted as quickly as possible, Newton assumed a domineering and condescending attitude toward Flamsteed. As president of the Royal Society, he used his influence with the government to be named as chairman of a body of "visitors" responsible for the Royal Observatory; then he tried to force the immediate publication of Flamsteed's catalogue of stars. The disgraceful episode continued for nearly 10 years. Newton would brook no objections. He broke agreements that he had made with Flamsteed. Flamsteed's observations, the fruit of a lifetime of work, were, in effect, seized despite his protests and prepared for the press by his mortal enemy, Edmond Halley. By court order, Flamsteed finally won his point and had the printed catalogue returned to him before it was generally distributed. He burned the printed sheets, and his assistants brought out an authorized version after his death. In this respect, and at considerable cost to himself, Flamsteed was one of the few men to beat Newton. Newton sought his revenge by systematically eliminating references to Flamsteed's help in later editions of *the Principia*.

The Principia immediately raised Newton to international prominence. In their continuing loyalty to the mechanical ideal, Continental scientists rejected the idea of action at a distance for a generation, but even in their rejection, they could not withhold their admiration for the technical expertise revealed by the work. Young British scientists spontaneously recognized him as their model. Within a generation, the limited number of salaries positioned for scientists in England, such as the chairs at Oxford, Cambridge, and Gresham College, was monopolized by the young Newtonians of the next generation. Newton, whose only close contacts with women were his unfulfilled relationship with his mother, who had seemed to abandon him, and his later guardianship of a niece, found satisfaction in the role of patron to the circle of young scientists. His friendship with Fatio De Duillier, a Swiss-born mathematician resident in London who shared Newton's interests, was the most profound experience of his adult life.

Almost immediately following the Principia's publication, Newton, a fervent if unorthodox Protestant helped to lead the resistance of Cambridge to James II's attempt to Catholicize it. Consequently, he was elected to represent the university in the convention that arranged the revolutionary settlement. In this capacity, he made the acquaintance of a broader group, including the philosopher John Locke. Newton tested the excitement of London life in the aftermath of the Principia. The great bulk of his creative work had been completed. He was never again satisfied with the academic cloister, and his desire to change was whetted by Fatio's suggestion that he find a position in London. Seek a place he did, especially through the agency of his friend, the rising politician Charles Montague, later Lord Halifax. Finally, in 1696, he was appointed warden of the mint. Although he did not resign his Cambridge appointments until 1701, he moved to London and subsequently centred his life there.

In the meantime, Newton's relations with Fatio had undergone a crisis. Fatio was taken seriously ill; then family and financial problems threatened to call him home to Switzerland. Newton's distress knew no limits. In 1693 he suggested that Fatio moves to Cambridge, where Newton would support him, but nothing came of the proposal. Though early 1693 the intensity of Newton's letters built almost palpably, and then, without surviving explanation, both the close relationship and the correspondence broke off. Four months later, without prior notice, Samuel Pepys and John Locke, both personal friends of Newton, received wild, accusatory letters. Pepys was informed that Newton would see him no more; Locke was charged with trying to entangle him with women. Both men were alarmed for Newton's sanity, and in fact, Newton had suffered at least his second nervous breakdown. The crisis passed, and Newton recovered his stability. Only briefly did he ever return to sustained scientific work, however, and the move to London was the effective conclusion of his creative activity.

As warden and then master of the mint, Newton drew a large income 2000 euros per annum. Added to his personal estate, the income left him a rich man at his death. The position, regarded as a sinecure, was treated otherwise by Newton. During the great recoinage, there was a need for him to be actively in command; even afterwards, however, he chose to exercise himself in the office. Above all, he was interested in counterfeiting. He became the terror of London counterfeiters, sending a good number to the gallows and finding in them a socially acceptable target on which to vent the rage that continued to well up within him.

Newton found time to explore other interests, such as religion and theology. In the early 1690's he had sent Locke a copy of a manuscript attempting to prove that Trinitarian passages in the Bible were latter-day corruptions of the original text. When Locke made moves to publish it, Newton withdrew in fear that his anti- Trinitarian views would become known. In his later years, he devoted much time to interpreting the prophecies of Daniel and St. John and to a closely related study of ancient chronology. Both works were published after his death.

Like most radical protestants, Newton was keenly interested in interpreting Biblical prophecy. However, he believed that God had specially chosen him to deliver the truth about how prophetic texts were to be understood.

A central plank of his general prophetic outlook was that images of the vials and trumpets described in the Book of Revelation referred to key events in the downfall of Raman Catholicism. In another remarkable treatise that can be dated to the late 1680s, Newton discussed what he believed would happen to the elect during Jesus' thousand-year reign immediately after his Second Coming. He suggested that Christ would reign with saints over a kingdom of mortals on earth that would continue to produce successive generations of people until the end of time.

Newton expanded vast energy researching the period before Christ, and he believed that there had once been a religion common to the entire world. In the first ages, he argued knowledge that the Earth was a planet circling the Sun was integrated into religious practices that involved worship around a central fire. Stonehenge was one of these sites. Newton also spent an astonishing amount of his time assessing how the simple original truths of Christianity had been corrupted. Picking up a theme central to his work on prophecy, he identified the fourth-century cleric Athanasius and his deviant associates as the vanguard of those who had introduced (as Newton saw it) the false religion of Catholicism and, in particular, the hideous doctrine of the Holy Trinity.

Despite the arrogance and occasionally rather mean behaviour he showed in his later life, Newton never lost the basic attitude towards Nature and 'Philosophy' that he had shown in his earlier years and his published work. Only a short time before his death, he made a remark that has since become an epitaph to this remarkable man and a testimonial to the spirit still animating theoretical physics today:

"I do not know what I may seem to the world, but as to myself, I seem to have been only like a boy playing on the seashore, and diverting myself in now and then finding a smoother pebble or prettier shell than ordinary, whilst the great ocean of truth lay undiscovered all before me"

Not much has changed since Newton's day in this regard- even though physics has advanced to a stage that Newton could have hardly imagined, it is even clearer now than it was then how little we understand.

Newton had interesting ideas about how 'philosophy' (which usually meant what would now be called physics) should be done. They were interesting mainly because although he was quite dogmatic about them, his strong empiricist views on method were clearly at constant war with his more mystical views on what was the goal of philosophy. To get a good look at the empiricist side of his views, one need look no further than the Principia, where he lays out rules for the correct pursuit of physics:

Rule I:

We are to admit no more causes of natural things than such as are both true and sufficient to explain their appearances. To this purpose the philosophers say that Nature does nothing in vain, and more is in vain when less will serve; for Nature is pleased with simplicity, and affects not the pomp of superfluous causes.

Rule II:

Therefore to the same natural effects we must, as far as possible, assign the same causes. As to respiration in a man and in a beast; the descent of stones in Europe and in America; the light of our culinary fire and of the sun; the reflection of light in the earth, and in the planets.

Rule III:

The qualities of bodies, which admit neither intensification nor remission of degrees, are found to belong to all bodies within reach of our experiments, are to be esteemed as the universal qualities of all bodies whatsoever. Since the qualities of bodies are only known to us by experiments, we are to hold for universal all such as universally agree with experiments; such as are not liable to diminution can never be quite taken away... The extension, hardness, impenetrability, mobility, and inertia of the whole, result from the extension, hardness, impenetrability, mobility, and inertia of the parts; hence we conclude the least particles of all bodies to be also extended, and hard and impenetrable, and movable, and endowed with their proper inertia. And this is the foundation of all philosophy.

Sir Isaac Newton

Rule IV:

In experimental philosophy we are to look upon propositions inferred by general induction from phenomena as accurately or very nearly true, not withstanding any contrary hypotheses that may be imagined, till such time as other phenomena occur, by which they may either be made more accurate, or liable to exceptions. This rule we must follow, that the argument of induction may not be evaded by hypotheses.

These remarks are very much in tune with the whole austere spirit of the Principia and its mechanical approach. Newton never abandoned them, even when trying to push some his much less secure views on light and the aether, for which he had in some cases very little experimental justification (let alone proof!). For example in his Opticks, published in 1704, he has a list of 'Queries' (which were nothing but the speculations in chapter of his old manuscript, disguised in a form which made them less controversial). One of the last of these, Query 31, added to the final edition, goes as follows:

'As in Mathematics, so in Natural Philosophy, the Investigation of difficult Things by the Method of Analysis, ought ever to precede the Method of Composition. This Analysis consists of making Experiments and Observations, drawing general Conclusions from them by Induction, and admitting no Objections against the Conclusions, but such as are taken from Experiments or other certain Truths.

Hypotheses are not to be regarded in Experimental Philosophy. And although the arguing from Experiments and Observations by Induction be no Demonstration of general Conclusions; yet it is the best way of arguing which the Nature of Things admits of, and maybe looked upon as so much the stronger, by how much the Induction is more general. And if no Exception occurs from Phenomena, the Conclusion may be pronounced generally. But if at any time afterwards, any Exception shall occur from Experiments, it may then begin to be pronounced with such Exceptions as occur. By this way of Analysis, we may proceed from Compounds to Ingredients, and from Motions to the Forces producing them; and in general, from Effects to their Causes, and from particular Causes to more general ones, till the Argument ends in the most general. This is the Method of Analysis: And the Synthesis consists in assuming the Causes discover'd, and establish'd as Principles, and by them explaining the Phenomena proceeding from them, and proving the Explanations'

This passage is very interesting to see alongside the speculations about what substance filled empty space and his answer that there must be some incorporeal but living and intelligent being of which space is the 'sensorium'.

There is no reason to believe that Newton was being either irrational or inconsistent here- he genuinely felt that one had to go to a non-mechanical explanation of the universe to understand what lay beneath the mere mechanical facts and rules about the motion of bodies. It seems rather that he saw the 'Experimental Philosophy' as a way of harnessing and controlling the speculative or 'hypothetical' approach to which he was so prone in order to keep speculation from running wild. In this, he was surely adopting the correct strategy- given how little the purely speculative approach had yielded in 2000 years of 'philosophizing'. However, one also feels that his Baconian view of how one proceeded by inferring hypotheses from the experiment was hardly a good description of how he really arrived at his conclusions (although he seemed to think it was).

There are many interesting things about this fascinating Englishman, from the job he held that involved sending people to the gallows to the cause of one of his most bitter rivalries. These are as follows:

- **His unhappy childhood helped shape his secretive personality.**

Newton was born prematurely on Christmas Day 1642 at his family's home, Woolsthorpe Manor, near the town of Grantham, England, several months after the death of his father, an illiterate farmer. When Newton was three, his mother wed a wealthy clergyman, Barnabas Smith, who didn't want a stepson. Newton's mother went to live with her new husband in another village, leaving behind her young son in the care of his grandparents. The experience of being abandoned by his mother scarred Newton and likely played a role in shaping his solitary, untrusting nature. As a teen, he made a list of his past sins and among them was: "Threatening my father and mother Smith to burn them and the house over them." Newton immersed himself in his work as an adult, had no hobbies, and never married. He even remained silent about some of his scientific and mathematical discoveries for years if he published them.

- **Newton's mother wanted him to be a farmer.**

At age 12, Newton was enrolled in a school in Grantham, where he boarded at the home of the local apothecary because the daily walk from Woolsthorpe Manor was too long. Initially, he wasn't a strong student; however, as the story goes, following a confrontation with a school bully, Newton started applying himself to best the other boy and transformed into a top student. However, at age 15 or 16, he was ordered to quit school by his mother (then widowed for a second time) and return to Woolsthorpe Manor to become a farmer. The teen was uninterested in the job and fared poorly at it. Eventually, Newton's mother was persuaded by her son's former headmaster in Grantham (where British Prime Minister Margaret Thatcher was born in 1925) to allow him to return to school. After finishing his coursework there, Newton left for Trinity College, the University of Cambridge, in 1661, putting farming behind him for good.

Sir Isaac Newton

- **The Black Death inadvertently set the stage for one of his most famous insights.**

In 1665, following an outbreak of the bubonic plague in England, Cambridge University closed its doors, forcing Newton to return home to Woolsthorpe Manor. While sitting in the garden there one day, he saw an apple fall from a tree, providing him with the inspiration to eventually formulate his law of universal gravitation. Newton later relayed the apple story to William Stukeley, who included it in a book, "Memoir of Sir Isaac Newton's Life," published in 1752.

In 2010, a NASA astronaut carried a piece of the ancient apple tree aboard the space shuttle Atlantis for a mission to the International Space Station. The Royal Society, a scientific organization once headed by Newton, loaned the piece of the tree for the voyage, as part of a celebration of the 350th anniversary of the group's founding.

Today, the original apple tree continues to grow at Woolsthorpe Manor.

- **As a professor at Cambridge, his lectures were poorly attended.**

In 1669, Newton, then 26, was appointed the Lucasian professor of mathematics at Cambridge, one of the world's oldest universities, whose origins date to 1209. (Newton was the second person to hold the Lucasian professorship; the 17th person, from 1979 to 2009, was physicist and "A Brief History of Time" author Stephen Hawking.) Although he remained at Cambridge for nearly 30 years, Newton showed little interest in teaching or in his students, and his lectures were sparsely attended; frequently, no one showed up at all. Newton's attention was centered on his own research.

- **Newton ran the Royal Mint and had forgers executed.**

In 1696, Newton was named to the job of warden of the Royal Mint, which was responsible for producing England's currency. He left Cambridge, his long-time home, and moved to his nation's capital city, where the mint was located in the Tower of London. Three years later, Newton was promoted to the more lucrative position of master of the mint, a post he held until his death in 1727. During his tenure at the Mint, Newton supervised a major initiative to take all of the country's old coins out of circulation and replace them with more reliable currency. He also was focused on investigating counterfeiters and, as a result, became acquainted with the city's seedy underbelly as he personally tracked down and interviewed suspected criminals, receiving death threats along the way. A number of forgers he went after were sent to the gallows.

- **Newton was deeply religious from a young age**

He felt compelled to jot down a list of his sins in one of his notebooks. Already a student at Trinity College at Cambridge University at the time, he divided these sins into acts that happened before and after Whitsunday 1662 or the seventh Sunday after Easter. Newton took even small lapses quite seriously, such as having unclean thoughts or using the Lord's name. The list also showed a darker side of Newton, including him making threats to burn his mother and stepfather in their home.

- **He had a serious interest in alchemy.**

In addition to the scientific endeavors for which he's best known, Newton spent much of his adult life pursuing another interest, alchemy, whose goals included finding the philosopher's stone, a substance that allegedly could turn ordinary metals like lead and iron into gold. He was secretive about his alchemical experiments and recorded some of his research in code.

Among his other research projects, Newton analyzed the Bible in an attempt to find secret messages about how the universe works.

- **Newton served in Parliament—quietly.**

From 1689 to 1690, Newton was a member of Parliament, representing Cambridge University. During this time, the legislative body enacted the Bill of Rights, which limited the monarchy's power and laid out the rights of Parliament along with certain individual rights. Newton's contributions to Parliament were limited; he reportedly spoke only once when he asked an usher to close a window because it was chilly. Nevertheless, while in London,

Newton became acquainted with several influential people, from King William III to the philosopher John Locke. Newton served a second brief term in Parliament from 1701 to 1702 and again seems to have contributed little.

- **He had fierce rivalries.**

When it came to his intellectual rivals, Newton could be jealous and vindictive. Among those with whom he feuded was German mathematician and philosopher Gottfried Leibniz; the two men had a bitter battle over who invented calculus. Newton developed a version of calculus in the 1660s but didn't publish his work. In the 1670s, Leibniz formulated his calculus version, publishing his work a decade later. Newton later charged that the German scholar had plagiarized his unpublished writings after documents summarizing them circulated through the Royal Society. Leibniz contended he'd reached his results independently and implied that Newton had stolen from his published work. To defend himself, Leibniz eventually appealed to the Royal Society, and in 1712, Newton, who'd served as the organization's president since 1703, agreed that an impartial committee would be assembled to look into the issue. Instead, he packed the committee with his supporters and even penned the group's report, which publicly credited him with discovering calculus. Today, however, Leibniz's calculus system is the one commonly used.

- **Newton got a career boost from the Great Plague of 1665**

He completed his bachelor's degree at Cambridge University's Trinity College in 1665 and wanted to continue his studies, but an epidemic of the bubonic plague soon altered his plans. The university closed its doors not long after the disease had begun its deadly sweep through London. During the first seven months of the outbreak, roughly 100,000 London residents had died.

Back at his family home, Woolsthorpe Manor, Newton actually began working on some of his most important theories. It was here that he explored ideas of planetary motion and made progress on his understanding of light and color. Newton may have also made advances in his theory about gravity by observing an apple fall from a tree in his garden.

- **Newton was knighted.**

In 1705, Newton was knighted by Queen Anne. By that time, he'd become wealthy after inheriting his mother's property following her death in 1679 and also had published two major works, 1687's "Mathematical Principles of Natural Philosophy" (commonly called the "Principia") and 1704's "Opticks." After the celebrated scientist died at age 84 on March 20, 1727, he was buried in Westminster Abbey, the resting place of English monarchs and such notable non-royals as Charles Darwin, Charles Dickens and explorer David Livingstone.

In old age, Newton's health deteriorated: when he was eighty, he began to suffer from incontinence due to a weakness in the bladder, and his movement and diet became restricted. He ate mainly vegetables and broth and was plagued by a stone in the bladder. In 1725 he fell ill with gout and endured haemorrhoids the following year. Meanwhile, the pain from his bladder stones grew worse, and on March 19, 1727, he blacked out, never to regain consciousness. He died on March 20, at the age of eighty-five, and was buried in Westminster Abbey; his funeral attended by all of England's eminent figures, and his coffin carried by noblemen. It was, a contemporary noted, a funeral fit for a king.

His fame only grew with his death. Decades later, the philosopher David Hume would write that Newton was "the greatest and rarest genius that ever arose for the adornment and instruction of the species." Alexander Pope, the great English poet, composed an epitaph: "Nature and Nature's laws lay hid in night; / God said, Let Newton be! and all was light." This was an exaggeration; Newton's achievement was not a burst of light against the darkness but rather one explosion among many in the progress of the Scientific Revolution. But his was the greatest explosion by far, and Newton's impact on the world of Western thought can be compared to the impact of figures like Plato, Aristotle, Galileo, and even Jesus. Not every idea he pursued led to a triumph; his mathematical systems proved somewhat less successful than those of Leibniz, and his endless writings on alchemy and theology languished and are now read only by biographers seeking to understand this complex, contradictory man better. But Newton's triumphs, and the universal principles they uncovered, found no parallels in the science of his time. As the French thinker Laplace remarked, a trifle regretfully, there was only one universe, so only one man could discover its "fundamental law." That law was gravity, and that man, for hundreds of years, was Isaac Newton.

In the end, of course, Laplace was proven wrong. In the 20th century, Albert Einstein would overturn the Newtonian understanding of the universe, showing that the things that Newton had considered absolute-- space, distance, time, motion--were, in fact, relative. Einstein would show that space and time were one fabric, known as "space-time," that the universe was a wider and more fantastic place than Newton had thought possible, one in which formulae and unified laws could no longer hold. And yet, perhaps these subsequently- discovered wonders would not have surprised the great scientist. As an old man, when asked for an assessment of his achievements, Newton replied: "I do not know what I may appear to the world; but to myself, I seem to have been only like a boy playing on the seashore, and diverting myself now and then in finding a smoother pebble or prettier shell than ordinary, while the great ocean of truth lay all undiscovered before me."

Newton's grave is in front of the choir screen, close to his monument. The Latin inscription on it reads:

Hic depositum est, quod mortale fuit Isaaci Newtoni.

This may be translated as:

Here lies that which was mortal of Isaac Newton.
Newton's Monument

Newton's monument stands in the nave against the choir screen, to the north of the entrance to the choir. It was executed by the sculptor Michael Rysbrack (1694-1770) to the designs of the architect William Kent (1685-1748). It was finished in August 1730 and unveiled the following year.

The monument is of white and grey marble. Its base bears a Latin inscription and supports a sarcophagus with large scroll feet and a relief panel. The relief depicts boys using instruments related to Newton's mathematical and optical work. One has a telescope, one is looking through a prism, and another is balancing the Sun and planets on a steelyard. Others depict Newton's activities as Master of the Mint (producing coin of the realm) - the figures carry pots of coins, and an ingot (bar) of metal is being put into a furnace.

Above the sarcophagus is a reclining figure of Newton, in classical costume, his right elbow resting on several books representing his great works. They are labelled (on the fore-edges) 'Divinity', 'Chronology', 'Opticks' [1704] and 'Philo. Prin. Math' [Philosophia

Fsamily pic

Naturalis Principia Mathematica, 1686-7)]. With his left hand, he points to a scroll with a mathematical design shown on it (the 'converging series'), held by two standing winged boys. The painting on this scroll had been erased or cleaned off in the early 19th century and was re-painted in 1977 from details in Newton's manuscripts. The background is a pyramid on which is a celestial globe with the signs of the Zodiac, the constellations, and the path of the comet of 1680. On top of the globe sits a figure of Urania (the muse of Astronomy) leaning upon a book. On either end of the base is his coat of arms, two shinbones in saltire, within a decorative cartouche.

The monument originally stood out against the flat front of the choir screen, but was enclosed within the present decorative arch when Edward Blore re-modelled the screen in 1834.

Inscription

The inscription reads:

H. S. E. ISAACUS NEWTON Eques Auratus, / Qui, animi vi prope divinâ, / Planetarum Motus, Figuras, / Cometarum semitas, Oceanique Aestus. Suâ Mathesi facem praeferente / Primus demonstravit: / Radiorum Lucis dissimilitudines, / Colorumque inde nascentium proprietates, / Quas nemo antea vel suspicatus erat, pervestigavit. / Naturae, Antiquitatis, S. Scripturae, / Sedulus, sagax, fidus Interpres / Dei O. M. Majestatem Philosophiâ asseruit, / Evangelij Simplicitatem Moribus expressit. / Sibi gratulentur Mortales, / Tale tantumque exstitisse / HUMANI GENERIS DECUS. / NAT. XXV DEC. A.D. MDCXLII. OBIIT. XX. MAR. MDCCXXVI

This can be translated as follows:

Here is buried Isaac Newton, Knight, who by the strength of mind almost divine, and mathematical principles peculiarly his own, explored the course and figures of the planets, the paths of comets, the tides of the sea, the dissimilarities in rays of light, and, what no other scholar has previously imagined, the properties of the colours thus produced. Diligent, sagacious and faithful, in his expositions of nature, antiquity and the holy Scriptures, he vindicated by his philosophy the majesty of God mighty and good and expressed the simplicity of the Gospel in his manners. Mortals rejoice that such and so great an ornament of the human race has existed! He was born on 25th December 1642 and died on 20th March 1726.

The poet, Alexander Pope, had written an epitaph for Newton, but this was not allowed to be put on the monument in the Abbey "Nature and Nature's laws lay hid in night: God said, Let Newton be! and all was light".

Newton's niece Catherine Barton married John Conduitt, whose monument is at the opposite end of the nave to Isaac's. Conduitt commissioned the Newton monument.

Oxford Dictionary of National Biography

History of Parliament Online

The scientists of Westminster Abbey by A. Rupert Hall, 1966

His birthplace, Woolsthorpe Manor, is open to the public National Trust

Conduitt's sketch for the guidance of the monument designer is in the *Keynes Library* at King's College, Cambridge

Kent's original drawing (altered by the sculptor) and Rysbrack's terracotta model are in the Victoria & Albert Museum, London

William Kent-designing Georgian Britain edited by Susan Weber (2014 exhibition catalogue)

Rysbrack's sculptors drawing is in the *British Museum* collection

A preliminary design by Rysbrack (differs from the finished monument) is at the Plymouth City Museum and Arts Gallery

CHRONOLOGY

YEARS	DESCRIPTION
1646	**January:** Hannah Newton remarries and moves away, leaving her son to be raised by an uncle.
1649	**January 30:** Charles I beheaded by Cromwell and the Puritans.
1653	Death of Hannah's second husband; she returns to live with Isaac, bringing three children with her from her second marriage.
1654	Newton enrolls in the Grantham Grammar School
1658	**September 3:** Death of Cromwell
1660	Charles II crowned King of England, Restoration begins
1661	Newton enrolls in Trinity College, Cambridge.

1662	**July:** Founding of the Royal Society
1665	Newton receives his bachelor of arts from Trinity College
1666	Fire in London. Outbreak of plague drives Newton to retire to his mother's home in Woolsthorpe. Newton conducts prism experiments, discovers spectrum of light; works out his system of "fluxions," precursor of modern calculus; begins to consider the idea of gravity.
1669	Newton appointed Lucasian Chair of Mathematics at Trinity, a position he will hold for the next thirty-four years
1672	**January 11:** Newton elected to the Royal Society February: ·Newton's paper on optics and his prism experiments sent to the Society. Rivalry with Hooke begins.
1670s	Newton works on the mathematics of gravitation in his home in Cambridge.
1674	Hooke writes book in which he suggests existence of "attractive powers," akin to gravity.
1679	Death of Hannah Newton

1684	**January:** Hooke discusses principle of inverse squares with Christopher Wren and Halley. August:Halley goes to visit Newton in Cambridge, where they discuss the principle inverse squares and its relationship with planetary orbits. November: Newton completes his calculations on gravity and shares them with Halley, who urges him to publish.
1685	**February:** Newton sends a brief treatise, Propositiones de Motu, to the Royal Society, outlining his findings.
1686	April: Newton presents the first book of the Principia to the Royal Society
1687	**September:** Publication of the complete Principia
1688-89	Glorious Revolution in England. James II flees to France, William and Mary take the throne.
1689	Newton elected as Cambridge's representative to Parliament.
1693	Newton's "Black Year." He is plagued by depression and insomnia, and apparently suffers a nervous breakdown in September.

1695	Newton appointed warden of the Mint, to oversee the implementation of a new currency. He leaves Cambridge and moves to London.
1699	Newton named master of the Mint.
1703	Death of Hooke; Newton elected President of the Royal Society.
1704	Publication of *Opticks*; beginning of feud with Leibniz.
1705	Newton knighted by Queen Anne
1712	Royal Society commission, under Newton's direction, investigates the competing claims of Leibniz and Newton to having developed calculus, and decides in favor of Newton.
1713	Second edition of the *Principia* published.
1714	**November 14:** Death of Leibniz
1726	Third edition of the *Principia* published; all reference to Leibniz has been removed.
1727	**March 20 :** Death of Sir Isaac Newton, in London.

Acknowledgement

I am grateful to God for giving me the courage to do, knowledge to understand, and will to attempt and take over the task of highlighting the important events, dates, incidents and contributions of Sir Isaac Newton.

I would like to express my gratitude and regards to one and all who helped me through the journey of this writing and always be supportive.

I want to thank all my readers for their time and devotion to read this book. You people are my real source of inspiration. Your support, views and recommendations encourage us to improve and keep on writing.

-Savneet Kaur